I AM
DAILY
AFFIRMATIONS

CHRISTINA CASH

Mission: To Proclaim Transformation and Truth
Publisher: Transformed Publishing, Cocoa, FL
Website: www.transformedpublishing.com
Email: transformedpublishing@gmail.com

This work is based on the author's life experiences, lifestyle, and personal Biblical study, not medical or mental health expertise.

Illustrations retrieved from Storyblocks.com by publisher (subscription plan March 2023).

Definition research conducted using Oxford English Dictionary, https://www.oed.com/ Retrieved Sept. & Oct. & 2023.

ISBN: 978-1-953241-54-2 (paperback)   ISBN: 978-1-953241-59-7 (hardcover)

Dedication

I dedicate this book to my children and grandchildren. May you always see yourself how God and I see you.

Acknowledgements

I must first give the highest praise to my Maker. Father God, where would I be without you? You get all the glory!

Much appreciation and thanks to my spiritual leaders, Pastor Errol Beckford and Teacher Oshowo. Thank you for always leading by example and teaching me how to live the right way, through Biblical principles.

This book belongs to

_____

Received on

20 _____

_____

From

_____

I AM Daily Affirmations

CHRISTINA CASH

"Have you commanded the morning since your days *began, and* caused the dawn to know its place, that it might take hold of the ends of the earth, and the wicked be shaken out of it?"
–Job 38:12-13

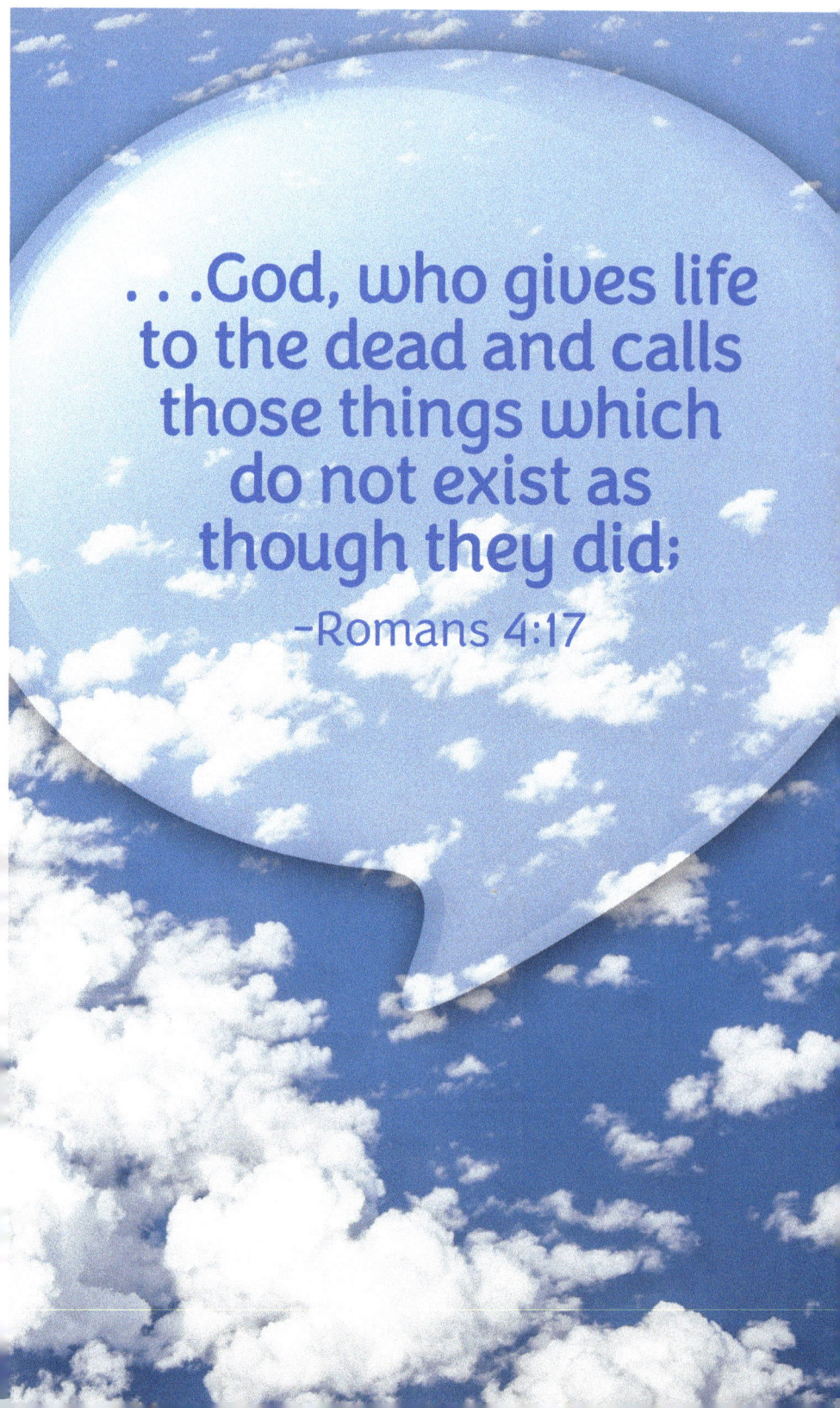

Table of Contents

What is your goal for, *I Am Daily Affirmations*?

_____
_____
_____
_____
_____
_____
_____
_____
_____
_____
_____
_____
_____
_____
_____
_____
_____
_____
_____
_____
_____
_____

Do you know who you are?

**Do you know what
you are capable of?**

Who are you?
What are you capable of?

Many people struggle when it comes to answering these questions or start to answer them with negativity. *Why?* It could be from never being confirmed by parents, being bullied, being mentally or physically abused, even guilt and shame from past mistakes.

Whatever it is, know that you don't have to keep being *that* person. Forgive yourself today and those who have hurt you. What's done is done. It cannot be changed. There is no time machine to go backwards so why do you keep trying to go there?

Let go and heal. Maybe you're thinking the pain is too deep but if I can do it, you can too. You have the inner strength to do so. You just need to find it. You have the power to change your mind about anything, including the thoughts you think about yourself. You are beautiful and priceless.

Do you know we are children of the Most High God?

And He wants us to know who we are in Him, not in the world. In this world we will be left to feel like we are less than, invaluable, disposable and unworthy, but we must rise above the status quo of what the world says and remember what our loving heavenly Father says about us. When you speak highly of yourself daily you are confirming what God already knows about you. You are perfectly and wonderfully made in His image. Speaking affirmations daily will help you become the person you've always known you could be but never tapped into. Proclaim who you are with encouragement from these alphabetized words and sayings. There are also some key Scriptures listed after the affirmations to meditate on daily. Do this every day for just two weeks and see the difference it makes in how you feel about yourself.

> For You formed my inward parts; You covered me in my mother's womb. I will praise You, for I am fearfully *and* wonderfully made; marvelous are Your works, and *that* my soul knows very well. My frame was not hidden from You, when I was made in secret, *and* skillfully wrought in the lowest parts of the earth. Your eyes saw my substance, being yet unformed. And in Your book they all were written, the days fashioned for me, when *as yet there were* none of them.
> -Psalm 139:13-16

Remember to say,
"I am,"
before each affirmation.

A

I am

Awesome,
At peace,
Above and
not beneath

Blessed are the peacemakers, for they shall be called sons of God.
-Matthew 5:9

And the Lord will make you the head and not the tail;
you shall be above only, and not be beneath, if you heed
the commandments of the Lord your God, which I
command you today, and are careful to observe them.
-Deuteronomy 28:13

B

I am

Blessed, Brilliant, and Bold in my faith in God

"The Lord bless you and keep you; the Lord make His face shine upon you, and be gracious to you; the Lord lift up His countenance upon you, and give you peace." '
-Numbers 6:24-26

[I]n whom we have boldness and access with confidence through faith in Him.
-Ephesians 3:12

And God gave Solomon wisdom and understanding beyond measure, and breadth of mind like the sand on the seashore, so that Solomon's wisdom surpassed the wisdom of all the people of the east and all the wisdom of Egypt.
-1 Kings 4:29-30 ESV

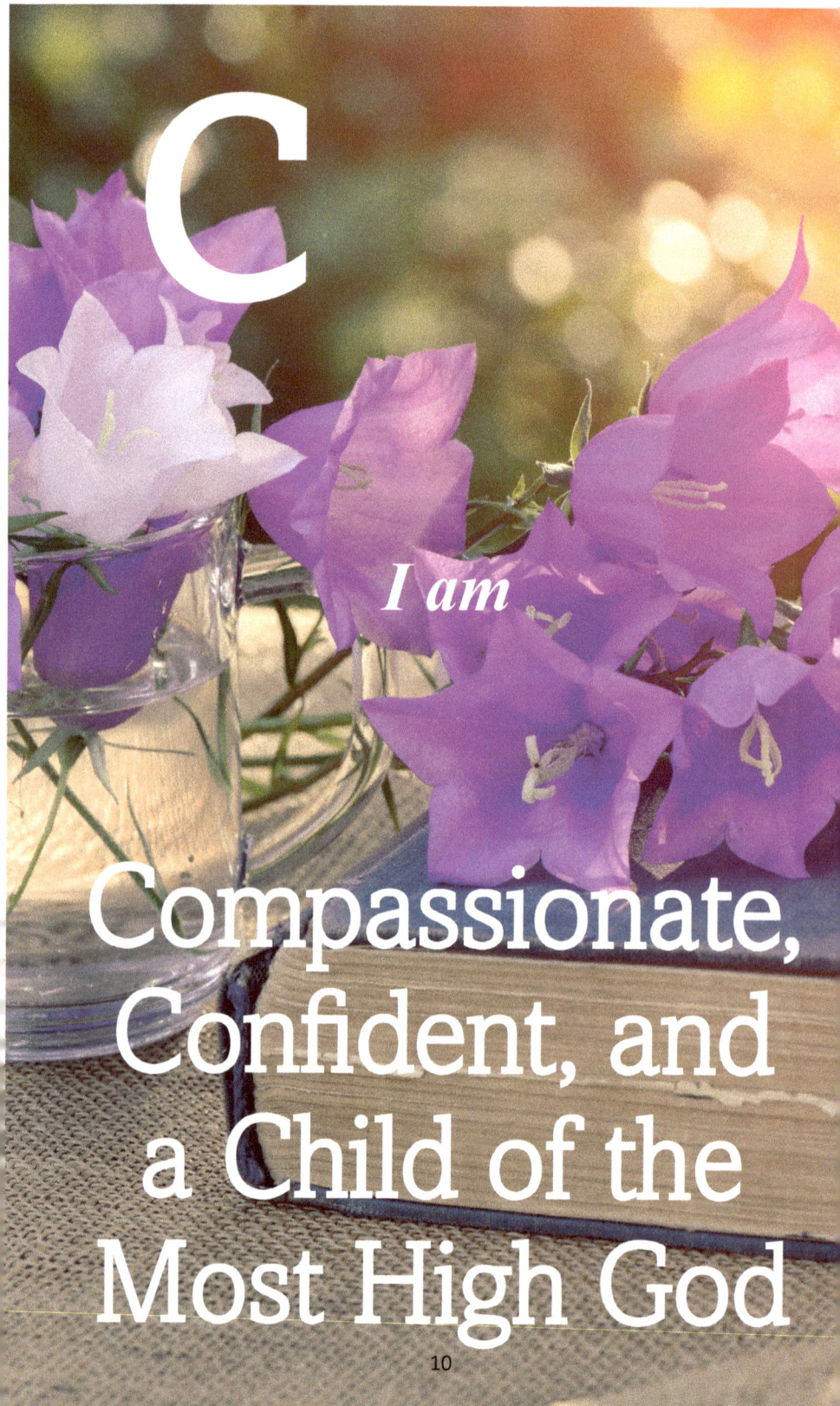

C

I am

Compassionate, Confident, and a Child of the Most High God

I said,
"You *are* gods, and all of you are children of the Most High.
-Psalm 82:6

Let Your compassion come to me, that I may live,
for Your law is my delight.
-Psalm 119:77 MEV

Such confidence we have through Christ toward God.
-2 Corinthians 3:4 NABRE

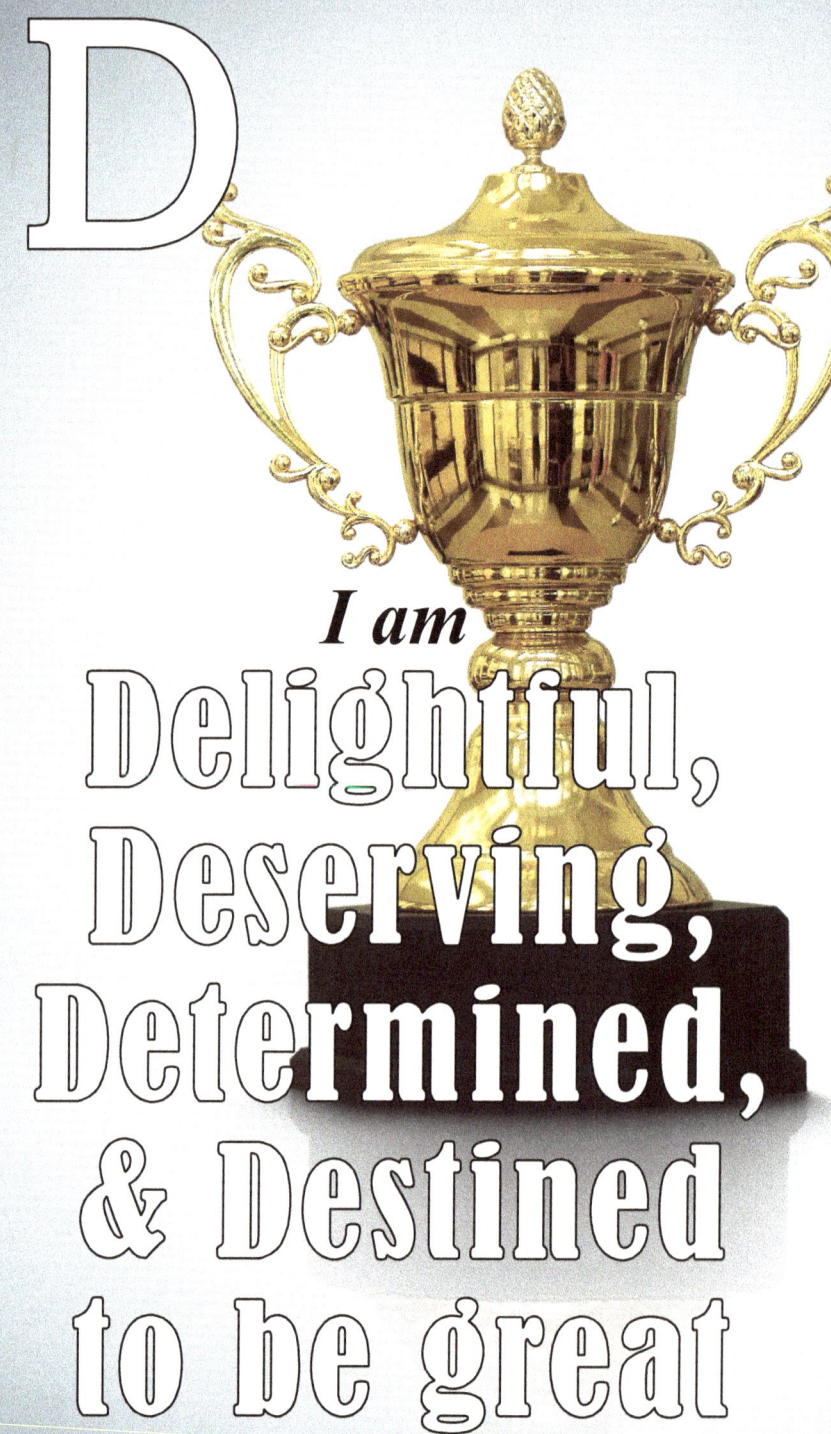

D

I am
Delightful,
Deserving,
Determined,
& Destined
to be great

He also brought me out into a broad place;
He delivered me because He delighted in me.
-Psalm 18:19

You shall increase my greatness,
And comfort me on every side.
-Psalm 71:21

Delight yourself also in the Lord,
And He shall give you the desires of your heart.
-Psalm 37:4

Every good gift and every perfect gift is from above,
and comes down from the Father of lights,
with whom there is no variation or shadow of turning.
-James 1:17

E

I am

Exquisite,
Exempt
from failure,
Equipped
and well able

For we are His workmanship,
created in Christ Jesus for good works,
which God prepared beforehand that we should walk in them.
-Ephesians 2:10

The Lord upholds all who fall,
And raises up all *who* are bowed down.
-Psalm 145:14

[T]hat the man of God may be complete,
thoroughly equipped for every good work.
-2Timothy 3:17

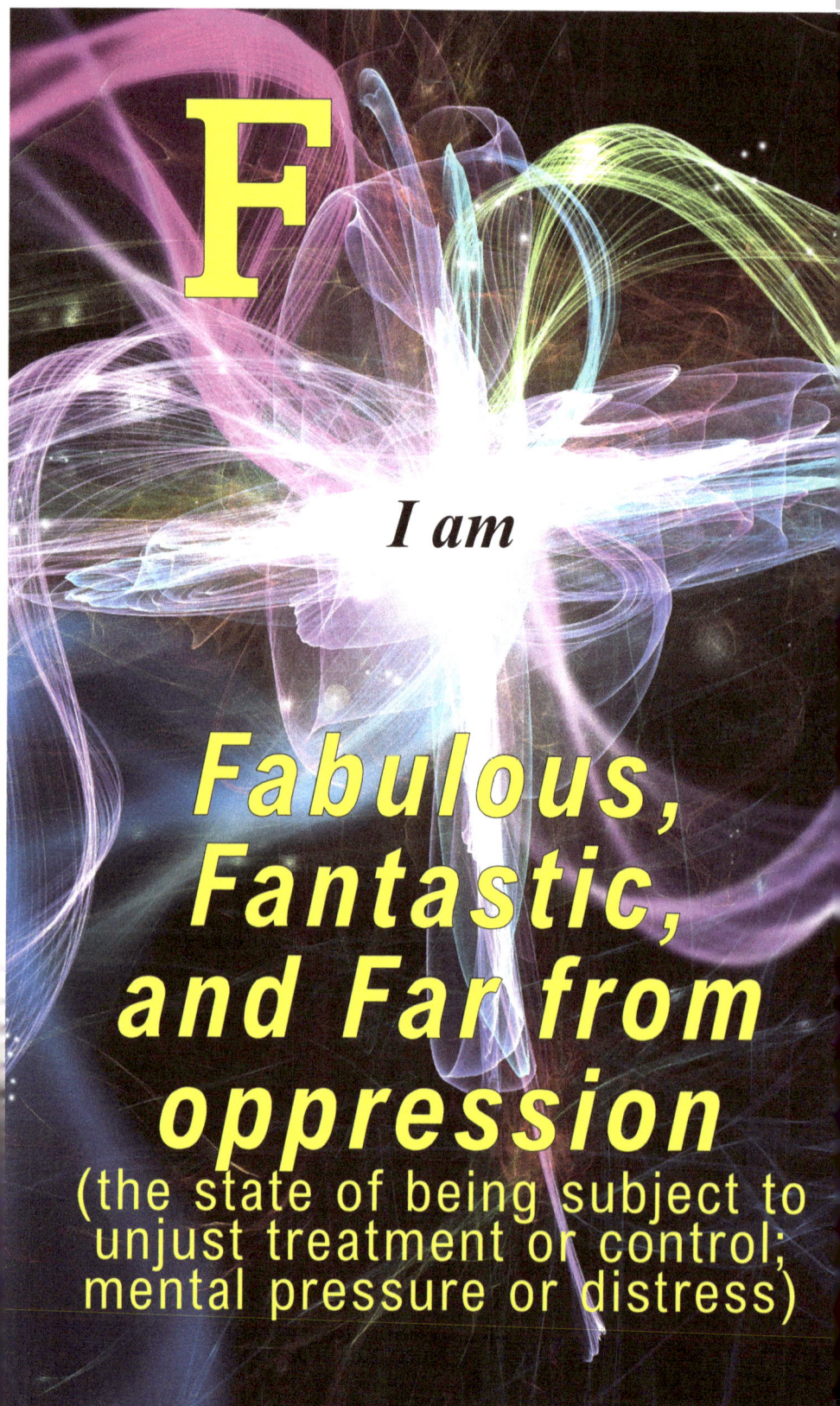

F

I am

Fabulous, Fantastic, and Far from oppression

(the state of being subject to unjust treatment or control; mental pressure or distress)

In righteousness you shall be established;
You shall be far from oppression, for you shall not fear;
And from terror, for it shall not come near you.
-Isaiah 54:14

Remember, O Lord, Your tender mercies
and Your lovingkindnesses, for they *are* from of old.
Do not remember the sins of my youth, nor my transgressions;
According to Your mercy remember me,
For Your goodness' sake, O Lord.
-Psalm 25:6-7

G

I am

GRACIOUS,
GRATEFUL,
AND GOD'S MOST
PRIZED POSSESSION

**[B]earing with one another and,
if one has a complaint against another, forgiving each other;
as the Lord has forgiven you, so you also must forgive.
-Colossians 3:13 ESV**

**He chose to give birth to us by giving us his true word.
And we, out of all creation, became his prized possession.
-James 1:18 NLT**

H

I am

Healthy, Hopeful, and Have the DNA of a winner

Behold, I will bring it health and healing; I will heal them and reveal to them the abundance of peace and truth.
-Jeremiah 33:6

['F]or the Lord your God *is* He who goes with you, to fight for you against your enemies, to save you.'
-Deuteronomy 20:4

I

I am

Intelligent, Irreplaceable, and Inclined to God's voice

So that you incline your ear to wisdom,
And apply your heart to understanding;
Then you will understand the fear of the Lord,
And find the knowledge of God.
-Proverbs 2:2, 5

J

I am

Joyful, Jazzy
(bright, colorful),
and a Jovial
(cheerful / friendly)
giver

Now may the God of hope fill you with all joy and peace in believing, that you may abound in hope by the power of the Holy Spirit.
-Romans 15:13

So let each one *give* as he purposes in his heart, not grudgingly or of necessity; for God loves a cheerful giver.
-2 Corinthians 9:7

K

I am

Keen

(Highly developed, sharp),

Knowledgeable

and

Kind-hearted

Be sober, be vigilant; because your adversary the devil walks
about like a roaring lion, seeking whom he may devour.
-1 Peter 5:8

For the Lord gives wisdom;
From His mouth *come* knowledge and understanding;
-Proverbs 2:6

Therefore, as the elect of God, holy and dearly loved,
clothe yourselves with a heart of mercy, kindness,
humility, gentleness, and patience,
-Colossians 3:12 NET

L

I am

Legendary,
Love/d/able,
& Lacking
nothing

For if you love those who love you, what reward have you?
Do not even the tax collectors do the same?
-Matthew 5:46

Let perseverance finish its work so that you may be mature
and complete, not lacking anything.
-James 1:4 NIV

M

I am
Magnificent, Motivated, and Made in the Image of God

So God created man in His *own* image; in the image of God
He created him; male and female He created them.
-Genesis 1:27

["]These things I have spoken to you, that in Me you may have peace.
In the world you will have tribulation; but be of good cheer,
I have overcome the world."
-John 16:33

N

I am

Noble
(having or showing fine personal qualities or high moral principles and ideals),

Nifty
(skillful, capable, useful),

and Nurturing
(help or encourage the development of)

But a noble person plans noble things;
he stands up for noble causes.
-Isaiah 32:8 CSB

Open your mouth, judge righteously,
And plead the cause of the poor and needy.
-Proverbs 31:9

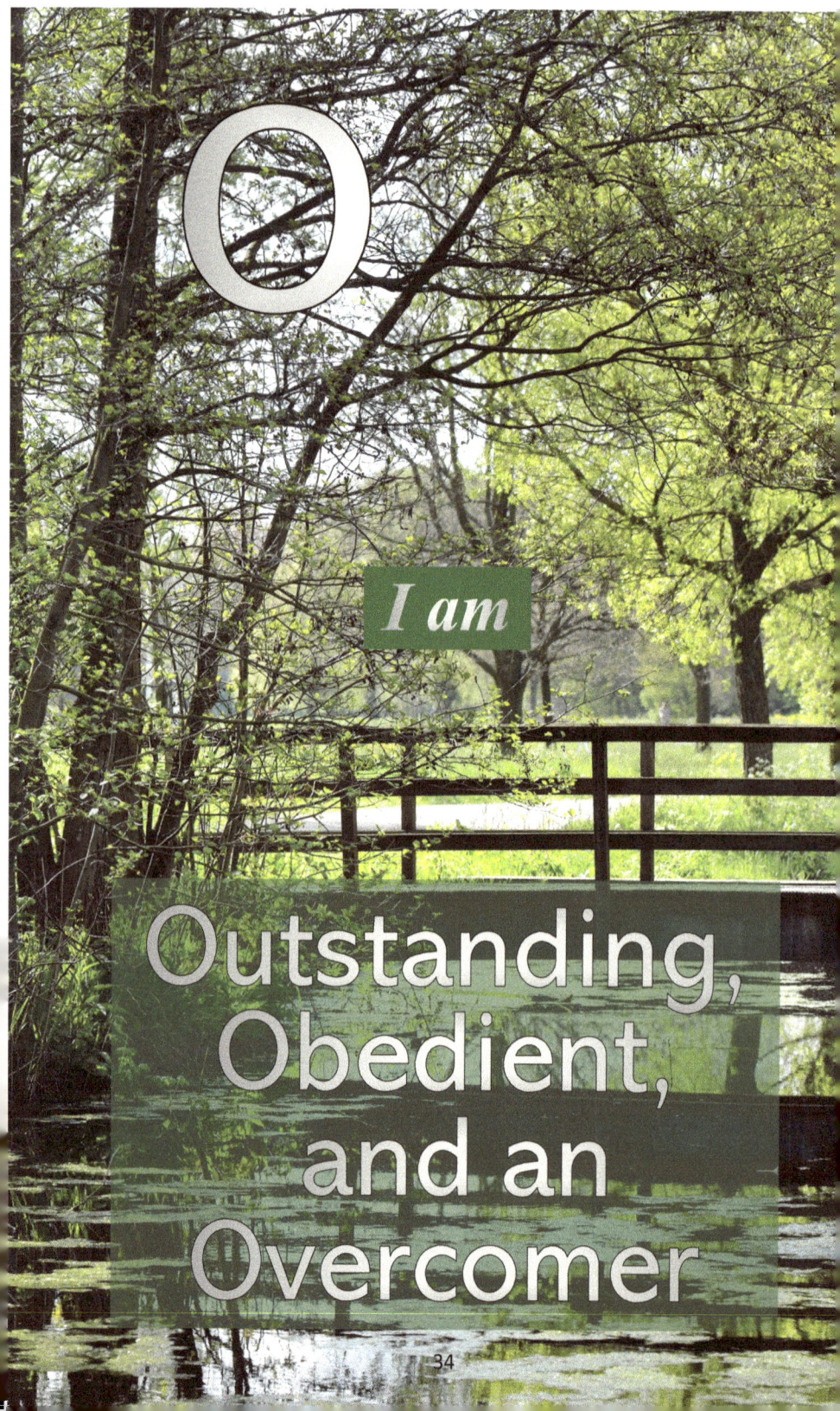

O

I am

Outstanding,
Obedient,
and an
Overcomer

**In fact, this is love for God: to keep his commands.
And his commands are not burdensome,
-1 John 5:3 NIV**

**For whatever is born of God overcomes the world.
And this is the victory that has overcome the world—our faith.
-1 John 5:4**

P

I am

Prosperous, Persistent, and Perfect in my imperfections

For I know what I have planned for you,' says the Lord.
'I have plans to prosper you, not to harm you.
I have plans to give you a future filled with hope.[']
-Jeremiah 29:11 NET

For You formed my inward parts;
You covered me in my mother's womb.
-Psalm 139:13

Q

I am

Quick-witted
(alert, sharp, quick thinking),

Quotable,

and Qualified

through Christ

["]Be always on the watch, and pray that you may be able
to escape all that is about to happen, and that you
may be able to stand before the Son of Man."
-Luke 21:36 NIV

Not that of ourselves we are qualified to take credit for anything
as coming from us; rather, our qualification comes from God,
-2 Corinthians 3:5 NABRE

[F]or I will give you a mouth and wisdom which
all your adversaries will not be able to contradict or resist.
-Luke 21:15

R

I am

Resilient
(able to withstand or recover quickly from difficult conditions),
Redeemed
(gain or regain possession of *something* in exchange for payment),
& Renewed
in my spirit through Jesus

Resist him, steadfast in the faith, knowing that the same
sufferings are experienced by your brotherhood in the world.
But may the God of all grace, who called us to His eternal
glory by Christ Jesus, after you have suffered a while,
perfect, establish, strengthen, and settle *you*.
-1 Peter 5:9-10

He has sent redemption to His people;
He has commanded His covenant forever:
Holy and awesome *is* His name.
-Psalm 111:9

S

I am
Strong,
Sunshine
to the darkness,
and **Sanctified**
(free from sin; purified)
through Christ

[B]ut they who wait for the Lord shall renew their strength;
they shall mount up with wings like eagles;
they shall run and not be weary;
they shall walk and not faint.
-Isaiah 40:31 ESV

Let your light so shine before men, that they may see
your good works and glorify your Father in heaven.
-Matthew 5:16

"Come now, and let us reason together,"
Says the Lord, "Though your sins are like scarlet,
They shall be as white as snow;
Though they are red like crimson,
They shall be as wool.
-Isaiah 1:18

T

I am

Transformed, Thriving, and Triumphant through the Lord

And do not be conformed to this world, but be transformed
by the renewing of your mind, that you may prove what
is that good and acceptable and perfect will of God.
-Romans 12:2
The righteous shall flourish like a palm tree,
He shall grow like a cedar in Lebanon.
-Psalm 92:12

But thanks be to God, who always leads us as captives in Christ's
triumphal procession and uses us to spread the aroma
of the knowledge of him everywhere.
-2 Corinthians 2:14 NIV

_____

_____

_____

_____

_____

_____

_____

_____

_____

_____

_____

_____

_____

_____

_____

_____

_____

_____

U

I am

UNFORGETTABLE,

UNSHAKEABLE,

& UNSTOPPABLE

He has made His wonderful works to be remembered;
The Lord *is* gracious and full of compassion.
-Psalm 111:4

Those who trust in the Lord are like Mount Zion,
which cannot be shaken but endures forever.
-Psalm 125:1 NIV

For a righteous man falls seven times, and rises again,
But the wicked stumble in *time of* disaster *and* collapse.
-Proverbs 24:16 AMP

V

I am

Valuable,
Virtuous,
and Validated
through Christ

Since you were precious in My sight,
You have been honored,
And I have loved you;
Therefore I will give men for you,
And people for your life.
-Isaiah 43:4

Do your best to present yourself to God as one approved,
a worker who has no need to be ashamed,
rightly handling the word of truth.
-2 Timothy 2:15 ESV

W

I am

Worthy, Wealthy, Wise

in my choices, and

Wonderfully

& fearfully made

Honor the Lord with your possessions,
And with the firstfruits of all your increase;
10 So your barns will be filled with plenty,
And your vats will overflow with new wine.
-Proverbs 3:9-10

I will praise You, for I am fearfully *and* wonderfully made;
Marvelous are Your works,
And *that* my soul knows very well.
-Psalm139:14

[B]ut test everything; hold fast what is good.
-1 Thessalonians 5:21 ESV

X

I am

Xenial
(friendly, hospitable),
an X-factor carrier
(a unique or special quality
that sets someone apart)
and eXcellent
in all things

She opens her mouth with wisdom,
And on her tongue *is* the law of kindness.
-Proverbs 31:26

You have been set apart as holy to the Lord your God,
and he has chosen you from all the nations
of the earth to be his own special treasure.
-Deuteronomy 14:2 NLT

Y

I am

Yielding success,
Youthful and vibrant,
and Yahweh's finest

In the morning sow your seed,
And in the evening do not withhold your hand;
For you do not know which will prosper,
Either this or that,
Or whether both alike will be good.

Rejoice, O young man, in your youth,
And let your heart cheer you in the days of your youth;
Walk in the ways of your heart,
And in the sight of your eyes;
But know that for all these
God will bring you into judgment.
-Ecclesiastes 11:6, 9

Z

I am

Zesty

(full of energy, enthusiasm and flavor-God says we are the salt of the earth!),

Zoetic

(being conscious and perceptive)

and **Zealous**

(enthusiastic in pursuit of)
for God

"You are the salt of the earth; but if the salt loses its flavor,
how shall it be seasoned? It is then good for nothing
but to be thrown out and trampled underfoot by men.["]
-Matthew 5:13

The way of fools seems right to them, but the wise listen to advice.
-Proverbs 12:15 NIV

Blessed *are* those who hunger and thirst for righteousness,
For they shall be filled.
-Matthew 5:6

_____

_____

_____

_____

_____

_____

_____

_____

_____

_____

_____

_____

_____

_____

_____

_____

_____

_____

The Challenge

You must speak it to the atmosphere! Even if you don't feel like it or see it manifesting yet. Say it daily until you believe it and see it come to pass. We were all made in the image of our maker, and He spoke our whole world into existence by the words of His mouth. So, if we were made in His image how much more so do you think our words will become evident that we speak?

I challenge you today to get up every morning and recite these affirmations out loud. You will start to feel like a champion, ready for whatever comes your way afterwards. You will be able to tell the world with confidence, "Bring it on!"

> For the word of God *is* living and powerful, and sharper than any two-edged sword, piercing even to the division of soul and spirit, and of joints and marrow, and is a discerner of the thoughts and intents of the heart.
> -Hebrews 4:12

> There is one who speaks like the piercings of a sword, But the tongue of the wise *promotes* health.
> -Proverbs 12:18

Be the wiser one and use your words to encourage not only yourself but others. Your mouthpiece is small but very powerful. And when it is misused, it could cause all sorts of chaos and strife and even block your blessings. I have been that person, talking out of emotion, hurt and anger. Therefore, I can tell you from my experiences, in many instances, if I had just kept my mouth shut things would not have been so bad.

Moreover, I know people who have talked their way right into the grave by continuously speaking about negative conditions they were diagnosed with. Listen up, God is the ultimate physician. I have overcome some illnesses myself. If I would've listened to what the doctor said and expected the negative outcome pronounced, I would be dead. But I wasn't having it. Not being a child of God. I know He is in the miracle working business. I've seen it myself. Now be advised, I am *not* saying to quit taking all your medications and give up your healthcare plan. God heals and performs miracles in different ways. One of those ways could be through medication and or a doctor. He may heal immediately or over time because He wants you to get something out of the process. The key is to *not* become faint and give up hope.

I know people who have complained about everyday life and then wondered why this or that has happened. It's because they kept talking about it until it manifested. We get what we speak and expect. The Bible says rain will fall on the just and unjust (*see* Matthew 5:45).

Not one of us is obsolete. So why waste the precious time God has given by being all upset and complaining about the inevitable? That's life. Why not speak life over death? What is there to lose? Nothing, but everything to gain.

In addition, ask God daily to reveal to you who you are through His Eyes. We don't have twenty / twenty vision when it comes to our lives. Our vision is blurred. Yet, our Heavenly Father sees everything clearly from beginning to end. Including our potential and talents. So, get out of your own way and partner with Him today by doing your part and letting Him do His. I promise you won't be disappointed. He will never mismanage you and it will be the best partnership you've ever had.

If you are reading this book and have not accepted Jesus into your heart, I highly recommend you do. You don't have to have a pastor pray over you. You just need to make the decision. Do you want the change and forgiveness that comes from having Jesus in your life? Believe God sacrificed Jesus for you and raised Him from the dead to save mankind from darkness. I can attest, it's the best decision I ever made. Say, "Lord, I repent of my sins and believe that You sent Your only begotten son to save me. Jesus, I accept You into my heart as my Lord and Savior, Amen."

> . . . "Worthy is the Lamb who was slain To receive power and riches and wisdom, And strength and honor and glory and blessing!"
>
> -Revelation 5:12

Congratulations! Immediately you have a friend for life in Jesus and your life will never be the same.

Now, don't think because you are saved that "poof" you're now going to be perfect - everything will be peachy and nothing trying will ever happen because that's simply not true. Nevertheless, what it does mean is you now acknowledge you have a partner in life who will never leave you nor give up on you. And instantly, He will go to work on your mind and heart and start instructing you in the way you should go, if you let Him because He is a gentleman and doesn't force Himself on you. This process is called sanctification, and it is a lifelong experience. Don't beat yourself up when you make mistakes. Just repent (ask for forgiveness and turn from your sins), get up, dust yourself off, and keep moving forward. You can do it!

Now that you know God has you covered from A-to-Z, start talking and walking in the victory. It's yours!

Additional Declarations

- I declare and decree, I am saved. I am forgiven through Christ. I am the righteousness of God (*see* 2 Corinthians 5:21).

- I am blessed, highly favored, and victorious.

- Royal blood flows through me. I am full of the fruits of the Spirit which are love, joy, peace, gentleness, kindness, meekness, endurance, and self-control (*see* Galatians 5:22).

- Greater is He who is in me than he who is in the world. I am not controlled by my flesh but by my spirit which is connected to the Holy Spirit (*see* John 14:12 & 1 John 4:4).

- I am healed by His stripes. I am free of sickness and disease. I am the head and never the tail. I am above and never beneath. I am a lender and not a borrower (*see* Isaiah 53:5 & Deu. 28:1-14).

- I am one of a kind. I am God's masterpiece. I am successful and everything I put my hands to the plow to do, I excel in (*see* Ephesians. 2:10, Luke 9:62, Genesis. 39:3, & Proverbs 22:9).

- I walk in excellence. I walk with integrity. I speak with skillful and godly wisdom, and on my tongue is the law of kindness. I am a people builder. I help call out their seeds of greatness and speak encouragement (*see* 1 Corinthians 14:12 & Colossians 3:23-24)

- My mind is sound. I have great understanding of things. My memory is sharp. I speak clearly and precisely. I listen before I speak or make decisions. I genuinely hear what God and others are saying and when it comes to what God wants me to do, I do it. I am focused. I am full of discernment. I am organized and I use my time wisely (*see* 2 Tim. 1:7, James 3:17, James 1:19-27, & Colossians 4:5).

- I reap what I sow, and I sow good seeds on good ground. Therefore, I harvest plenty. I speak only good things over my life, my children's lives, my children's children's lives, family, friends, and even foes. I am focused, not only on my own miracles, but becoming someone else's miracle. Therefore, good things happen in my life (*see* Galatians 6:7-8, John 12:50, 1 Peter 3:9-11, Isaiah 54:13, Deu. 7:9, Psalm 100:5, & James 2:15-17).

- I do not fear because God is with me. I trust in Him. He is my confidant. He is my defender. He is my rock and refuge. My fortress and my deliverer (*see* Isaiah 41:10, Psalm 27:1-3, Psalm 68:1-6, Psalm 62:7, Psalm 18:2, & Psalm 31:1-5).

- I am bold. I am courageous. I move swiftly like a deer and run my race. I overcome every obstacle that I face because I do my part and let the Lord take control and do His. God is on my side. And in my weakness His strength is made perfect. Hallelujah! (*see* Psalm 138:3, Joshua 1:7 -9, 2 Samuel 22:33-35, 1 Corinthians 9:24, Hebrews 12:1, Mathew 19:26, Romans 8:31-39, Psalm 18:32, & 2 Corinthians 12:9).

Pray with me:

Father, I receive every good thing
You have in store for me and
believe I will see it come to pass
in this lifetime, in Your perfect timing.

Help me to stay faithful to and stand on
Your word and on these words I have
spoken. I shake the wickedness out of
the day and every evil thought or word
that doesn't come from You.

I know You love me and only want
good for me. Thank You, Father.
In Jesus Name,
Amen.

You got this and God's got you!
NOW, GO BE GREAT!

I would have lost heart,
unless I had believed
That I would see the goodness of
the Lord In the land of the living.
-Psalm 27:13

About the Author

Christina Cash is the director of SWITCH (Stop Wasting Important Time Choose Him) International - teenage youth ministries at Celebration Tabernacle Church in Cocoa, FL.

She is also a part of GLOW (Glorious Life Outreach Worldwide) Ministries and a volunteer for the International Prayer Calls Network, standing on and praying for total universal revival worldwide, twenty-four hours a day.

Christina was born in Charlotte, NC but grew up around the east coast of Central Florida and currently resides in Merritt Island, FL.

Connect with Christina by email:

Christinacashministriesintl@gmail.com

Like and Follow Christina on Facebook:

Christina Cash Intl.

Get Connected

Glorious Life Outreach Worldwide (GLOW USA)

Sundays Services | 4pm (online)

Tuesday Word Feasts | 6pm (online)

**https://us05web.zoom.us/j/83072854416?
pwd=iReIY1o7iOaa4hsMkHE9qYQ16bPnen.1**

Or Scan:    **Password: GLOW**

International Prayer Calls Entry Link:
https://forms.gle/cRKC3GzQRJZviptAA

Or Scan:

80-Hours Prayer and Fasting on Telegram:
https://t.me/PrayerCalls

Or Scan:

GLORIOUS LIFE OUTREACH WORLDWIDE

GLOW

+234-705-403-8167 glowgloriously glowgloriously glowgloriously